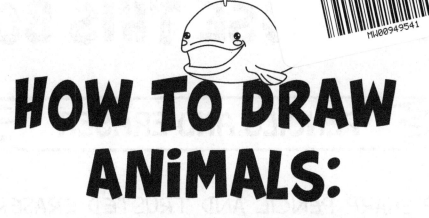

# HOW TO DRAW ANIMALS:

## 300 DRAWINGS OF SWEET PETS, EXOTIC & FARM FRIENDS, FANTASY BEINGS AND OTHER AMAZING CREATURES | BOOK FOR KIDS

ISBN: 979-8342987516

# HOW TO USE THIS BOOK

## PENCILS AND ERASER

GET YOUR SHARP PENCIL AND TRUSTED ERASER SET FOR A SMOOTH DRAWING EXPERIENCE. IF YOU WANT TO ADD A DASH OF COLOR TO YOUR CREATION, COLORED PENCILS ARE YOUR BEST CHOICE.

## 4-STEP EXAMPLE OF HOW TO DRAW

WHEN DRAWING WITH YOUR PENCIL, USE GENTLE LINES TO KEEP THE SKETCH CLEAN AND MAKE CORRECTING MISTAKES EASIER. TRACE LIGHTLY AND FOLLOW THE ARROWS TO FINISH YOUR PIECE. AFTERWARDS, USE THE BLANK SPACE TO EXPERIMENT AND PERFECT YOUR DRAWING SKILLS ON YOUR OWN.

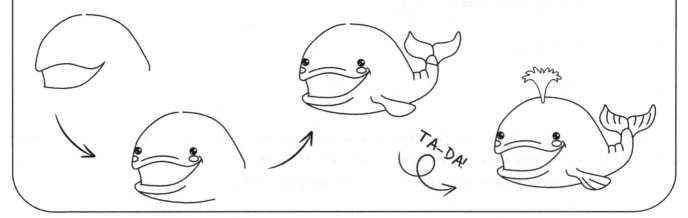

TA-DA!

# CONTENTS

## PETS, FARMS, AND DOGS

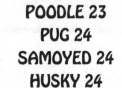
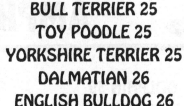
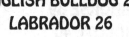

# FOREST ANIMALS

DEER 27
SQUIRREL 27
CUB 28
HEDGEHOG 28
FOX 28
TURTLE 29
DOE 29
RACCOON 29
MOOSE 30
WOLF 30
REINDEER 30
GRIZZLY BEAR 31

WILD BOAR 31
MARTEN 31
MARMOT 32
YAK 32
OPOSSUM 32
FAWN 33
SKUNK 33
FALLOW DEER 33
HARE 34
ELK 34
BLACK BEAR 34
WEASEL 35

CHAMOIS 35
BADGER 35
COYOTE 36
CHITAL 36
LIZARD 36
MOLE 37
OCELOT 37
ALPINE GOAT 37
BISON 38
MOUFLON 38
BOBCAT 38

# AQUATIC AND AMPHIBIAN ANIMALS

DOLPHIN 39
SEAHORSE 39
AXOLOTL 40
NARWHAL 40
OCTOPUS 40
STARFISH 41
WHALE 41
CRAB 41
HAMMERHEAD SHARK 42
JELLYFISH 42
ORCA 42
SALMON 43
CLOWNFISH 43
CACHALOT 43
LOBSTER 44

SAILFISH 44
SQUID 44
SHRIMP 45
BELUGA WHALE 45
STINGRAY 45
SWORDFISH 46
CRAYFISH 46
ANGELFISH 46
FLYING FISH 47
WHITE SHARK 47
MORAY EEL 47
PIRANHA 48
COD 48
SEASHELL 48
STURGEON 49

CORAL 49
PIKE 49
CLAM 50
CARP 50
MANATEE 50
PUFFERFISH 51
BLUEFIN TUNA 51
SEA LION 51
BARRACUDA 52
HALIBUT 52
SPOTTED GRUNTER 52
MOLA-MOLA 53
CROCODILE 53
WALRUS 53
SEA TURTLE 54

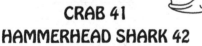

FROG 54
BEAVER 54
SEA OTTER 55

ALLIGATOR 55
SALAMANDER 55
NEWT 56

PLATYPUS 56
SEAL 56

# EXOTIC ANIMALS

ZEBRA 57
ELEPHANT 57
LION 58
HIPPO 58
GIRAFFE 58
ANTELOPE 59
CHIMPANZEE 59
KOALA 59
CAMEL 60
CHAMELEON 60
RHINO 60
GORILLA 61
SLOTH 61
TIGER 61
HYENA 62
KANGAROO 62
LLAMA 62
PUMA 63
POLAR BEAR 63
PYTHON 63
SCORPION 64
PANDA 64
ARMADILLO 64
LEOPARD 65

ORANGUTAN 65
IGUANA 65
IMPALA 66
CHEETAH 66
DINGO DOG 66
JAGUAR 67
TASMANIAN DEVIL 67
GIBBON 67
KOMODO DRAGON 68
SURICATE 68
BLACK CAIMAN 68
TAPIR 69
CAPUCHIN MONKEY 69
OKAPI 69
KOOKABURRA 70
AUSTRALIAN TAIPAN 70
ARABIAN ORYX 70
LEOPARD GECKO 71
FENNEC FOX 71
PORCUPINE 71
CLOUDED LEOPARD 72
PROBOSCIS MONKEY 72
GHARIAL 72
BACTRIAN CAMEL 73

MONITOR LIZARD 73
GNU GOAT 73
HONEY BADGER 74
AFRICAN PENGIUN 74
AFRICAN BUFFALO 74
WARTHOG 75
ANTEATER 75
AFRICAN WILD DOG 75
PANGOLIN 76
JAPANESE MACAQUE 76
THORNY DEVIL 76
CHINCHILLA 77
BABOON 77
AADVARK 77
CAPYBARA 78
GAZELLE 78
EGYPTIAN COBRA 78
JACKAL 79
TOPI 79
MANDRILL 79
WILDEBEEST 80
MARABOU STORK 80
RED PANDA 80

# BiRDS, FLiES, AND iNSECTS

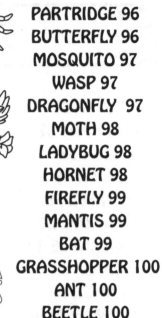

# MYTHiCAL AND FANTASY CREATURES

# PETS, FARMS, AND DOGS

**PUPPY**

**PRACTICE**

**CAT**

**PRACTICE**

## PARROT

TA-DA!

## HAMSTER

TA-DA!

## BUNNY

TA-DA!

# CANARY

# GUINEA PIG

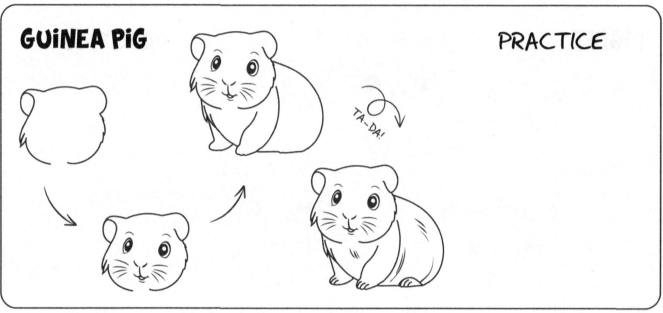

# GOLDFISH

## FERRET

TA-DA!

## PiGLET

TA-DA!

## DUCKLING

TA-DA!

# KiTTEN

# MOUSE

# CHiCK

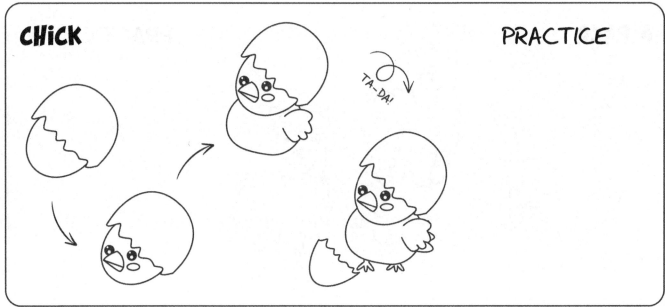

## CALF

## HORSE

## ALPACA

# LAMB

# GOAT

# DONKEY

## CHICKEN

TA-DA!

## COW

TA-DA!

## TURKEY

TA-DA!

**BULL**

**RABBIT**

**GOOSE**

## PiG

TA-DA!

## SNAiL

TA-DA!

## ROOSTER

TA-DA!

## SHEEP

TA-DA!

## DUCK

TA-DA!

## PHEASANT

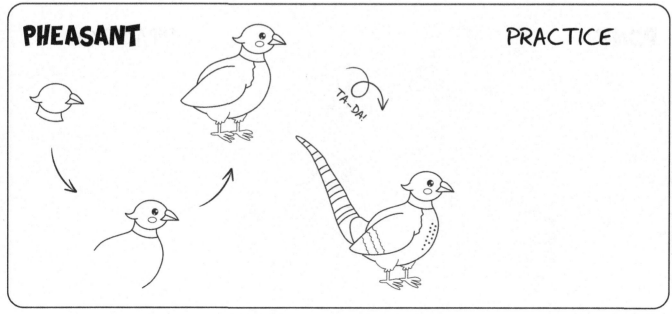

TA-DA!

## BEE

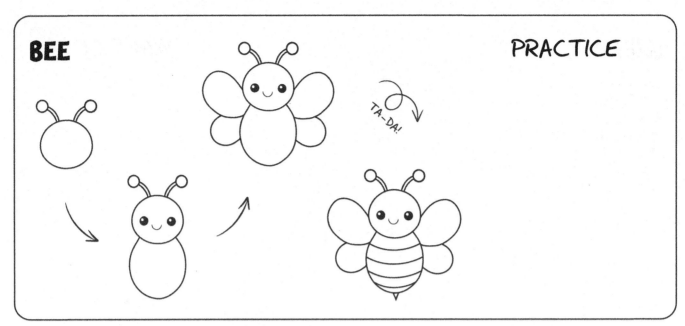

TA-DA!

## QUAIL

TA-DA!

## PONY

TA-DA!

## WELSH CORGI

## DACHSHUND

## DOBERMAN

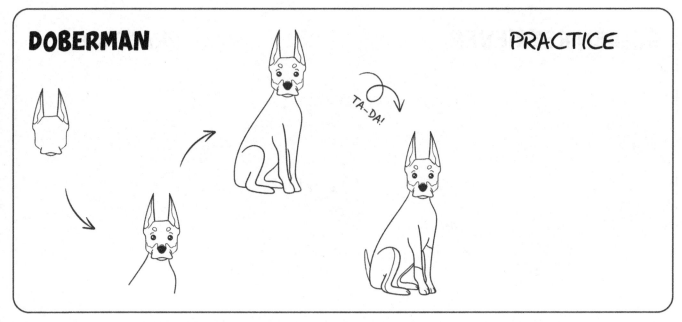

## FRENCH BULLDOG

## GERMAN SHEPHERD

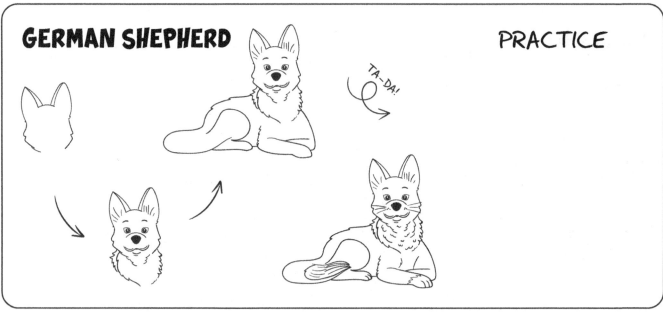

## GOLDEN RETRIEVER

## CHIHUAHUA

TA-DA!

## BORDER COLLIE

TA-DA!

## AFGHAN HOUND

TA-DA!

# GREAT DANE

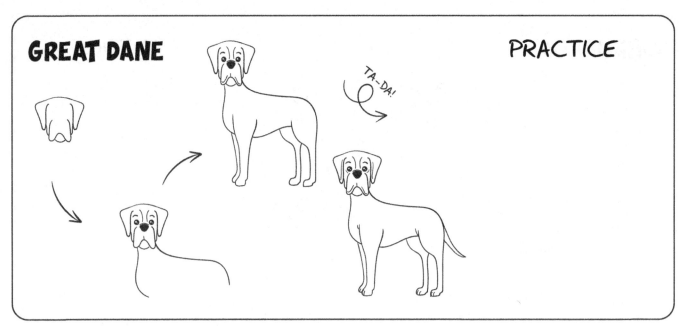

# JACK RUSSELL TERRIER

# MALTESE DOG

## MINIATURE SCHNAUZER

TA-DA!

## POMERANIAN

TA-DA!

## POODLE

TA-DA!

# PUG

# SAMOYED

# HUSKY

## BULL TERRIER

## TOY POODLE

## YORKSHIRE TERRIER

# DALMATIAN

TA-DA!

# ENGLISH BULLDOG

TA-DA!

# LABRADOR

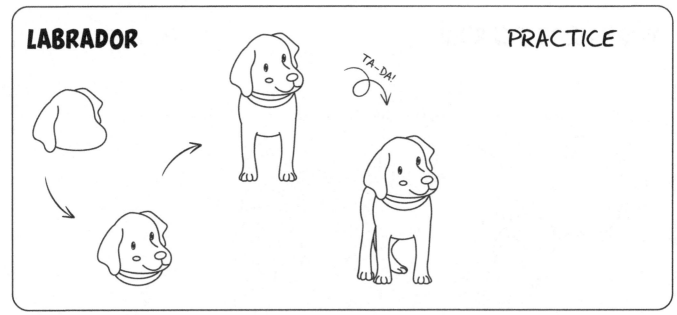

TA-DA!

# FOREST ANIMALS

## DEER

PRACTICE

TA-DA!

## SQUIRREL

PRACTICE

TA-DA!

## CUB

TA-DA!

## HEDGEHOG

TA-DA!

## FOX

TA-DA!

## TURTLE

TA-DA!

## DOE

TA-DA!

## RACCOON

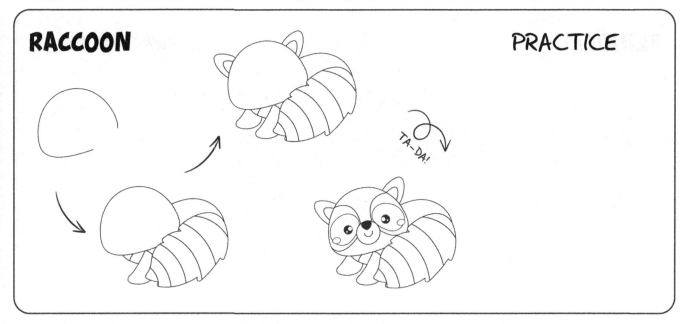

TA-DA!

## MOOSE

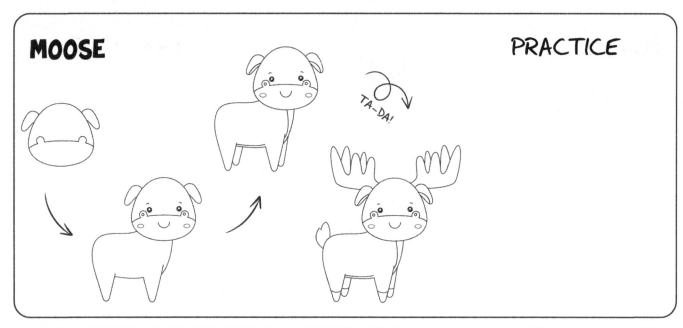

## WOLF

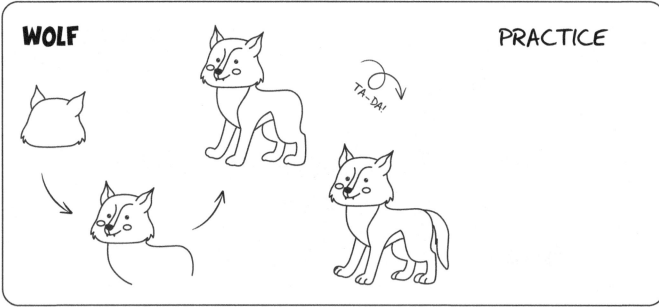

## REINDEER

## GRIZZLY BEAR

TA-DA!

## WILD BOAR

TA-DA!

## MARTEN

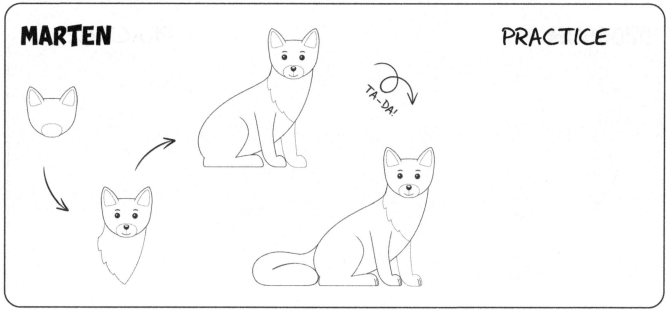

TA-DA!

**MARMOT**

TA-DA!

**YAK**

TA-DA!

**OPOSSUM**

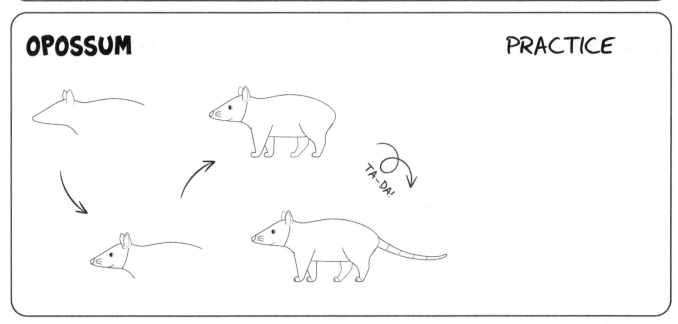

TA-DA!

## FAWN

TA-DA!

## SKUNK

TA-DA!

## FALLOW DEER

TA-DA!

# HARE

# ELK

# BLACK BEAR

## WEASEL

TA-DA!

## CHAMOIS

TA-DA!

## BADGER

TA-DA!

## COYOTE

## CHITAL

## LIZARD

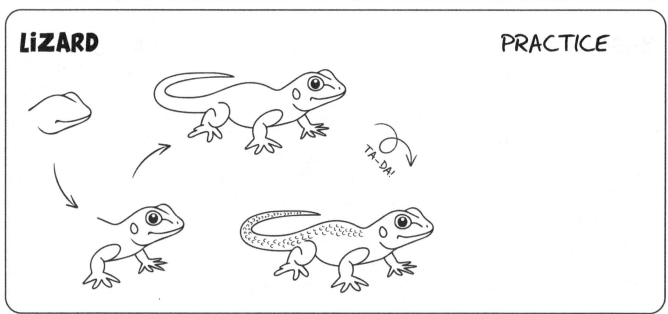

## MOLE

TA-DA!

## OCELOT

TA-DA!

## ALPINE GOAT

TA-DA!

## BISON

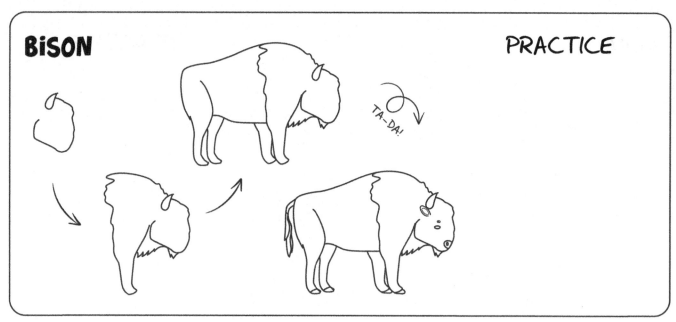

TA-DA!

## MOUFLON

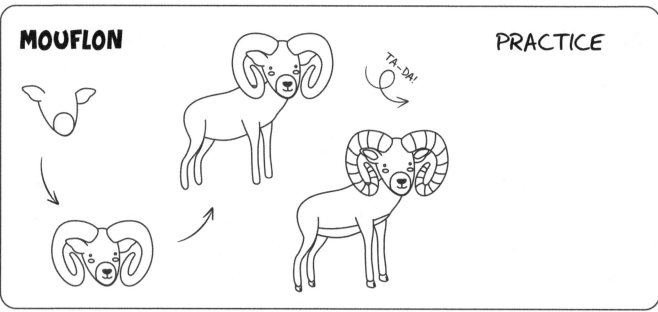

TA-DA!

## BOBCAT

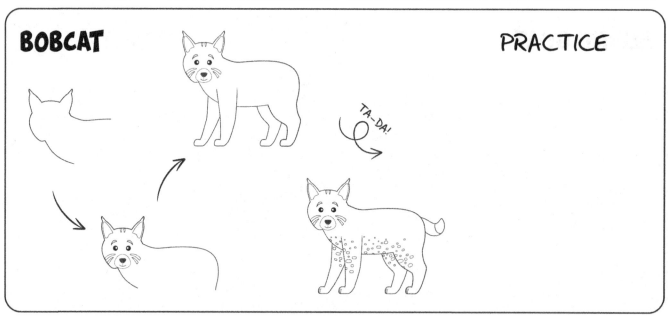

TA-DA!

# AQUATIC AND AMPHIBIAN ANIMALS

## DOLPHIN PRACTICE

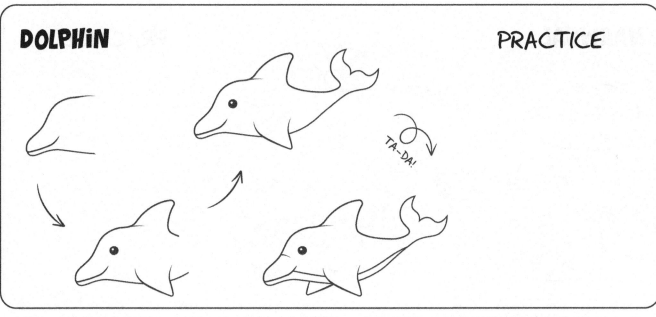

## SEAHORSE PRACTICE

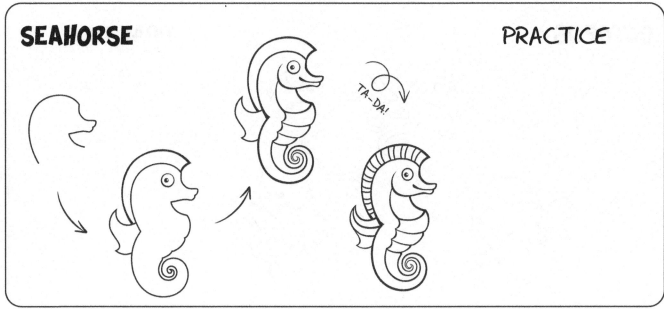

## AXOLOTL

## NARWHAL

## OCTOPUS

## STARFISH

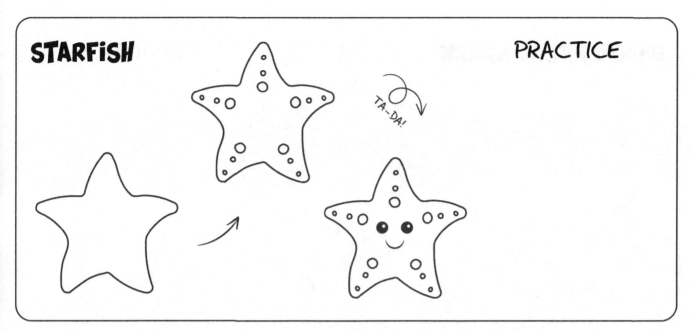

## WHALE

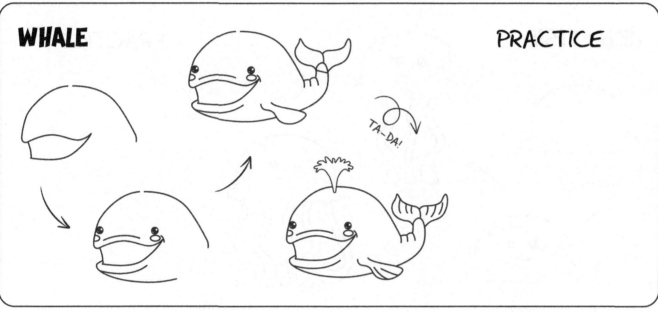

## CRAB

## HAMMERHEAD SHARK

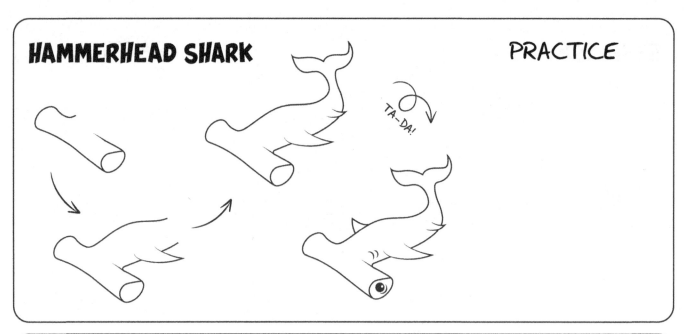

TA-DA!

## JELLYFISH

TA-DA!

## ORCA

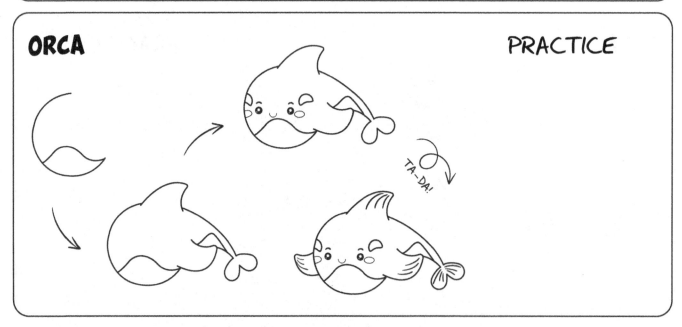

TA-DA!

## SALMON

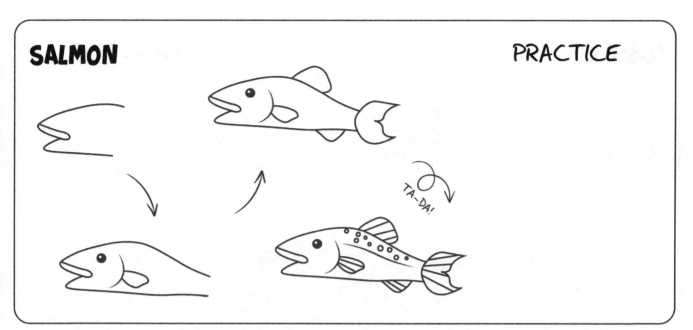

TA-DA!

## CLOWNFISH

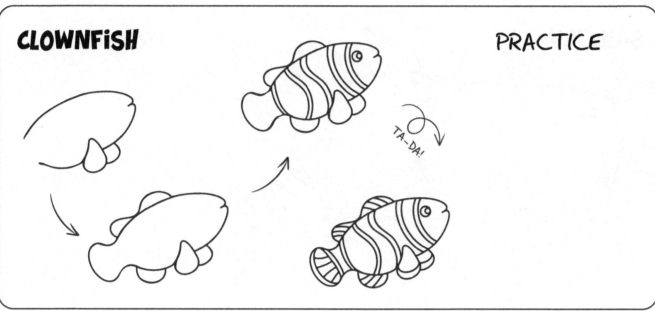

TA-DA!

## CACHALOT

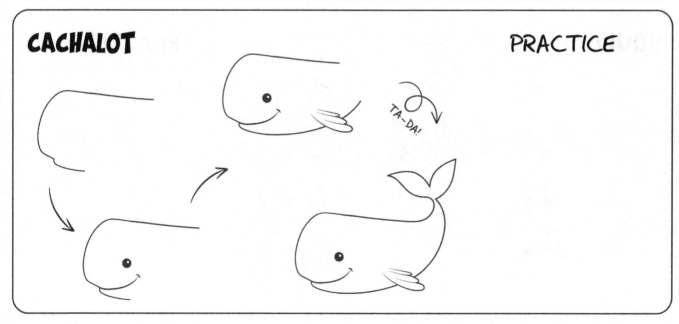

TA-DA!

## LOBSTER

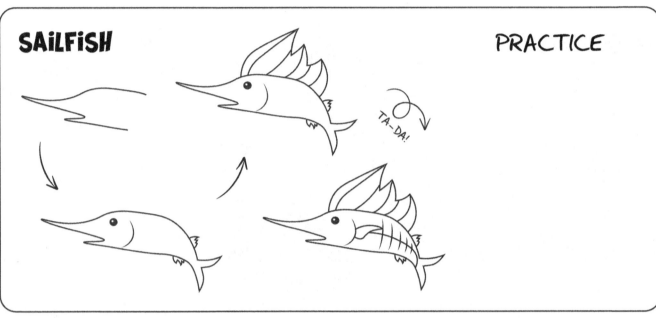

TA-DA!

## SAILFISH

TA-DA!

## SQUID

TA-DA!

# SHRIMP

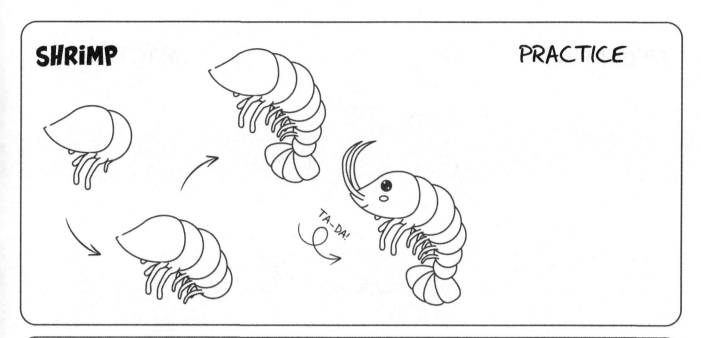

# BELUGA WHALE

# STINGRAY

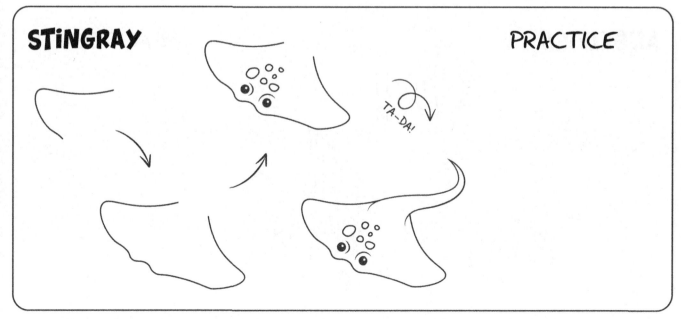

## SWORDFISH

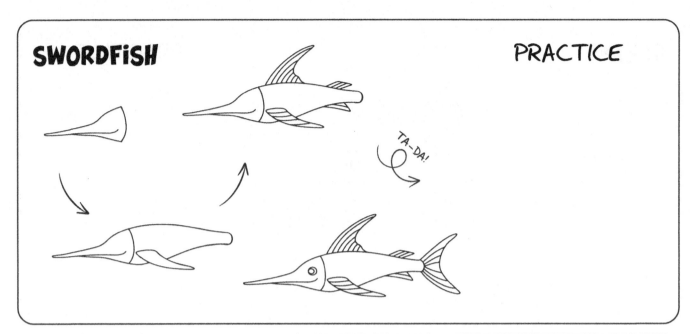

## CRAYFISH

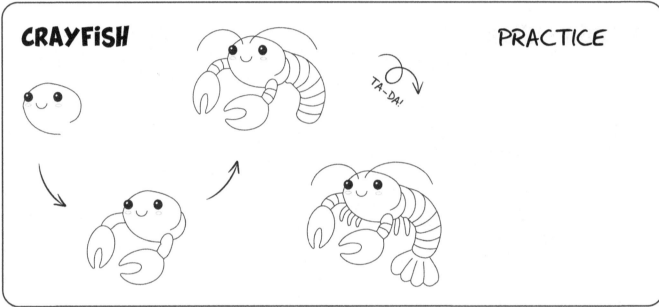

## ANGELFISH

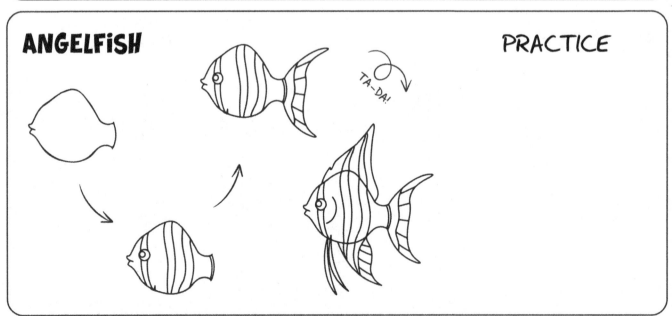

## FLYING FISH

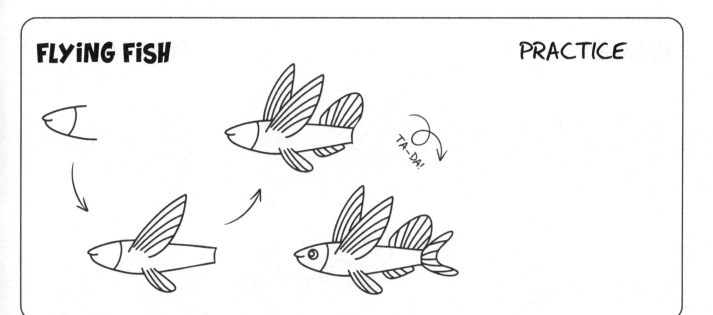

## WHITE SHARK

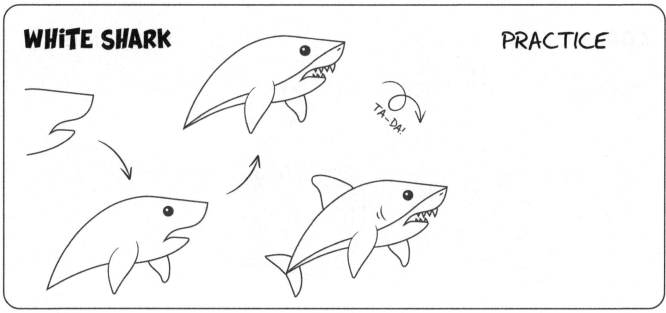

## MORAY EEL

## PIRANHA

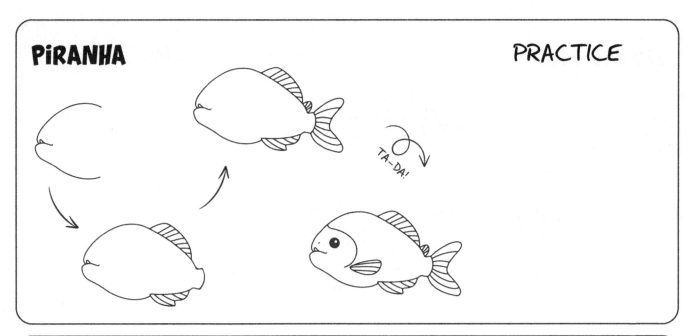

## COD

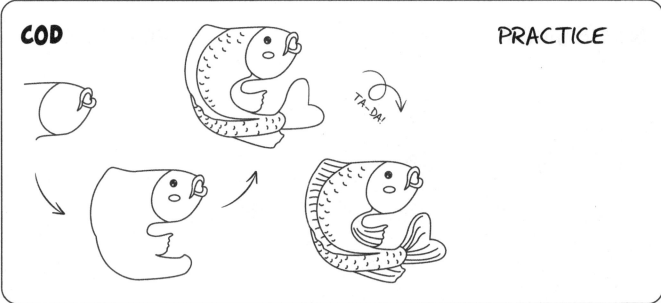

## SEASHELL

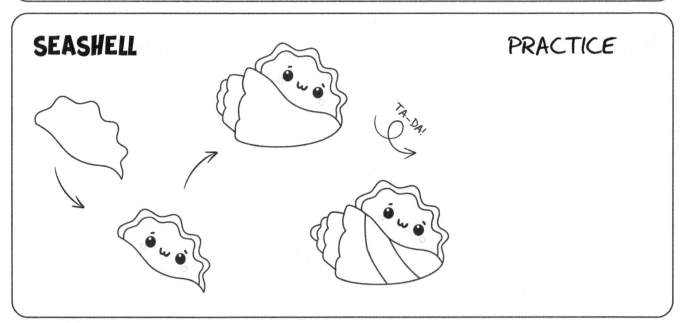

# STURGEON

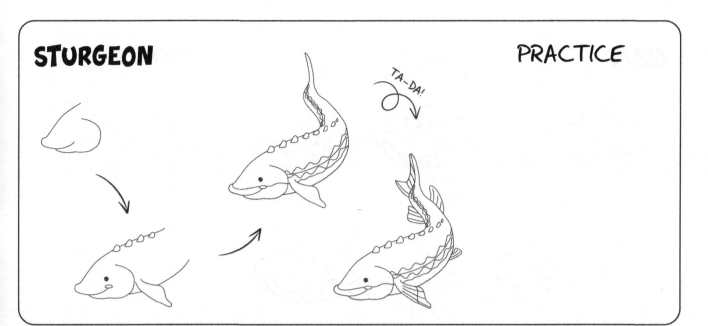

# CORAL

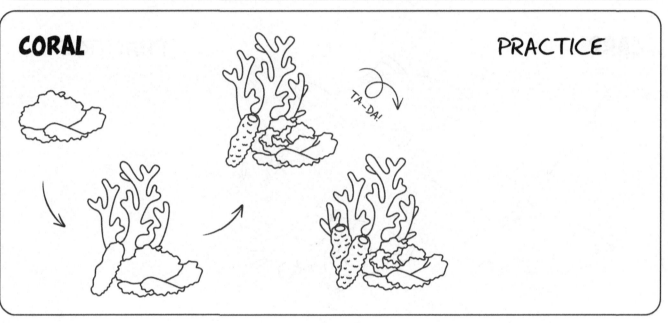

# PIKE

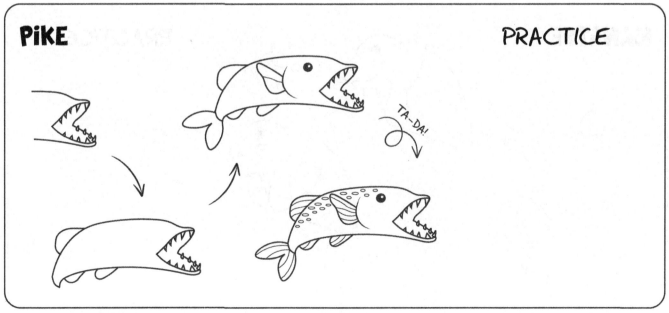

## CLAM

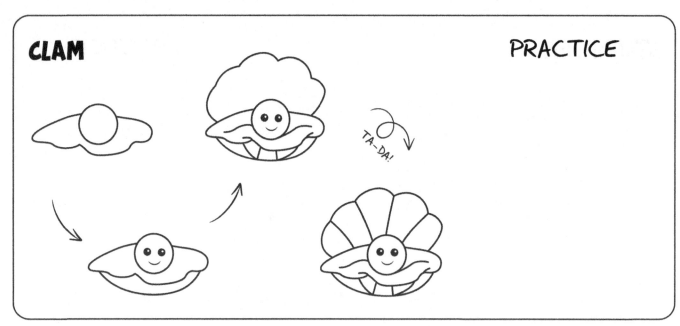

TA-DA!

## CARP

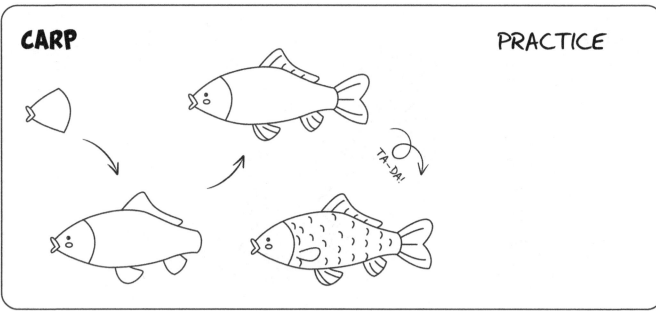

TA-DA!

## MANATEE

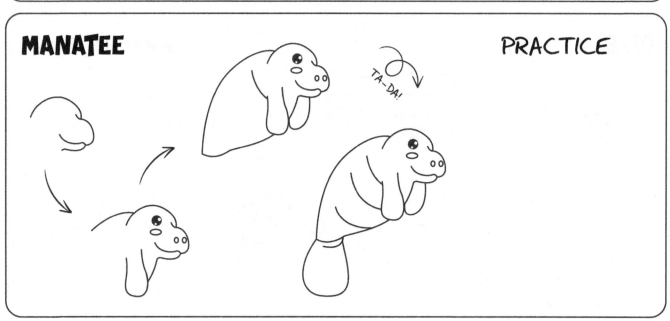

TA-DA!

## PUFFERFISH

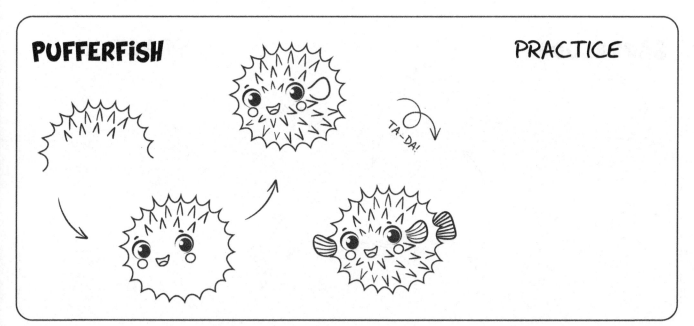

## BLUEFIN TUNA

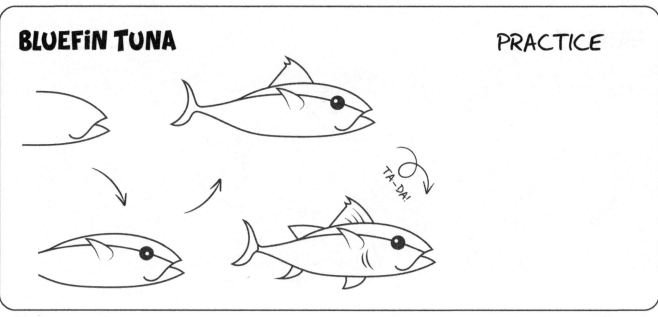

## SEA LiON

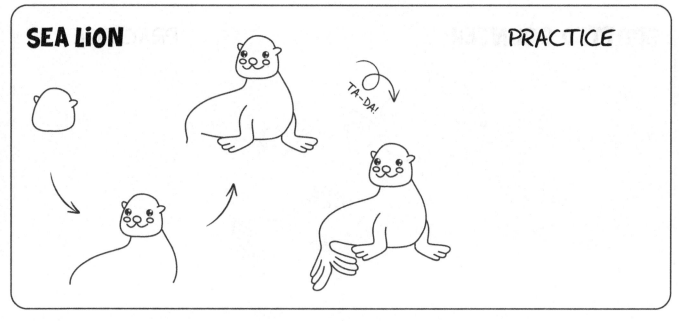

## BARRACUDA

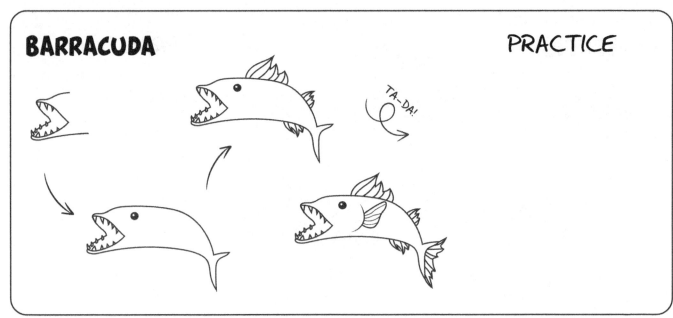

## HALIBUT

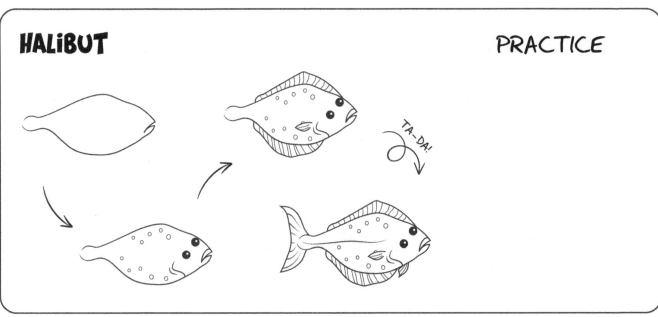

## SPOTTED GRUNTER

## MOLA-MOLA

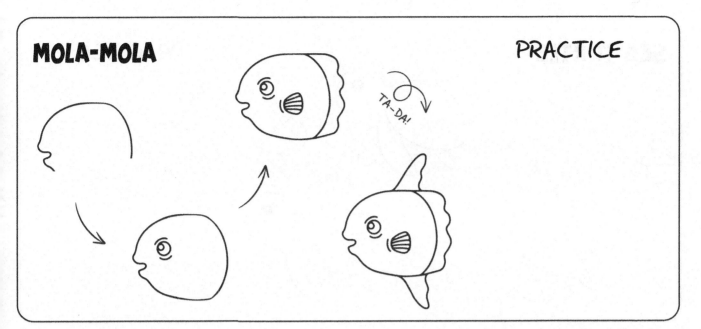

## CROCODILE

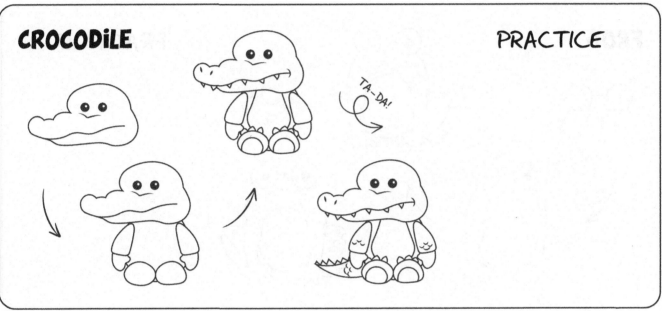

## WALRUS

## SEA TURTLE

TA-DA!

## FROG

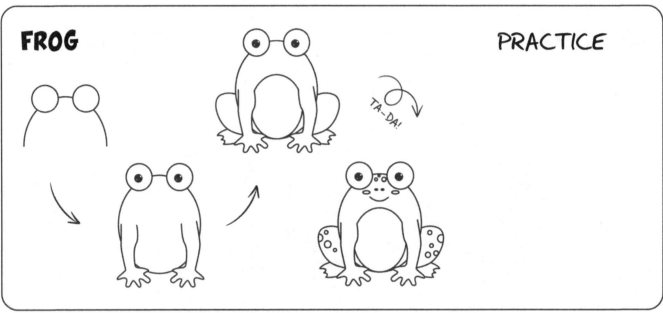

TA-DA!

## BEAVER

TA-DA!

## SEA OTTER

## ALLIGATOR

## SALAMANDER

## NEWT

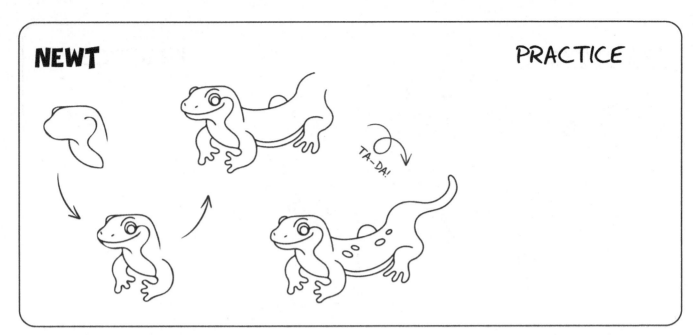

TA-DA!

## PLATYPUS

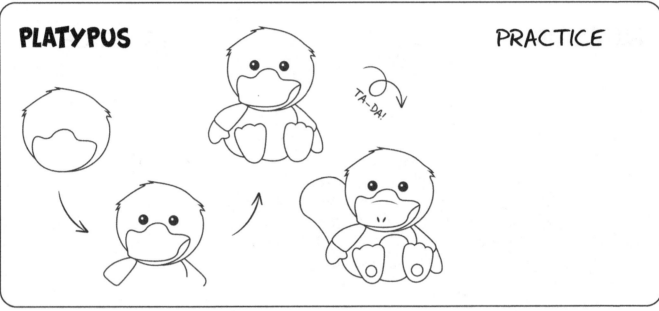

TA-DA!

## SEAL

TA-DA!

# EXOTIC ANIMALS

## ZEBRA PRACTICE

## ELEPHANT PRACTICE

**LiON**

TA-DA!

**HiPPO**

TA-DA!

**GiRAFFE**

TA-DA!

# ANTELOPE

# CHIMPANZEE

# KOALA

# CAMEL

# CHAMELEON

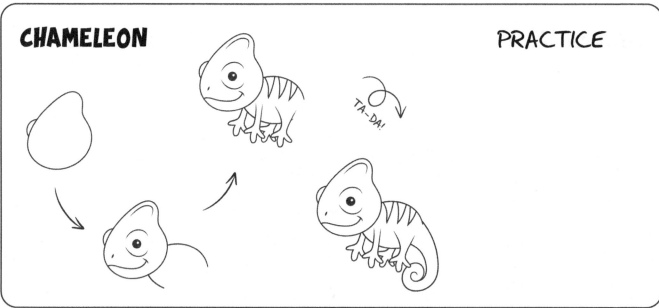

# RHINO

# GORILLA

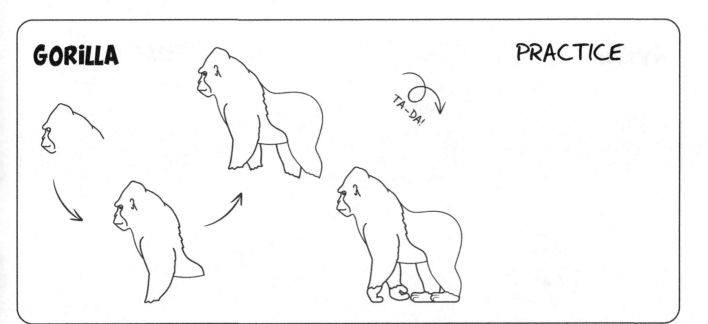

TA-DA!

# SLOTH

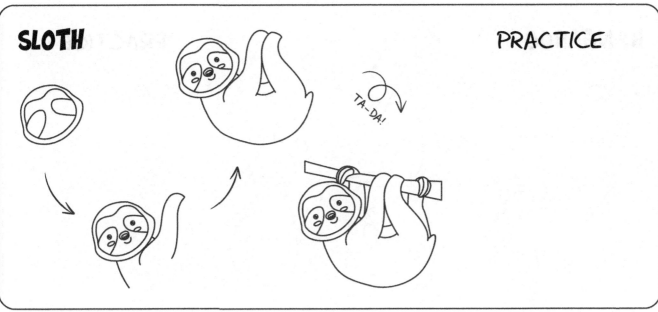

TA-DA!

# TIGER

TA-DA!

## HYENA

## KANGAROO

## LLAMA

# PUMA

# POLAR BEAR

# PYTHON

## SCORPION

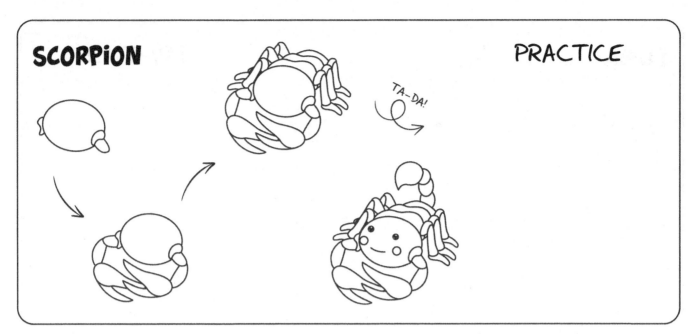

TA-DA!

## PANDA

TA-DA!

## ARMADILLO

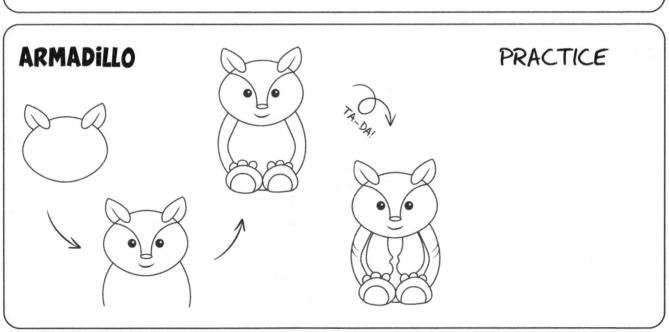

TA-DA!

## LEOPARD

## ORANGUTAN

## iGUANA

# iMPALA

# CHEETAH

# DiNGO DOG

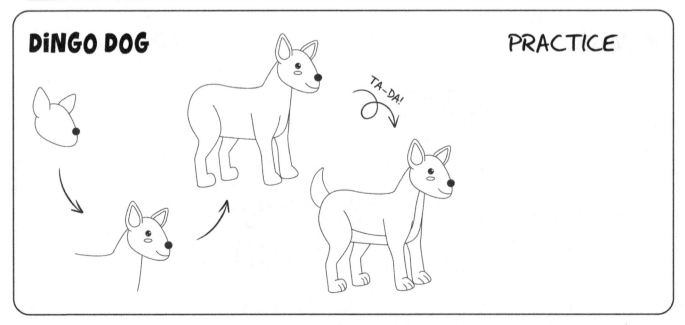

## JAGUAR

TA-DA!

## TASMANIAN DEVIL

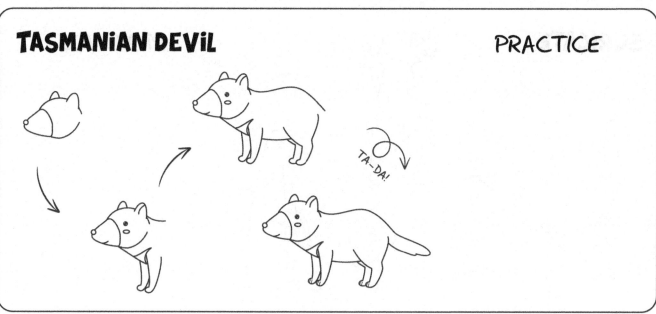

TA-DA!

## GIBBON

TA-DA!

# KOMODO DRAGON

TA-DA!

# SURICATE

TA-DA!

# BLACK CAIMAN

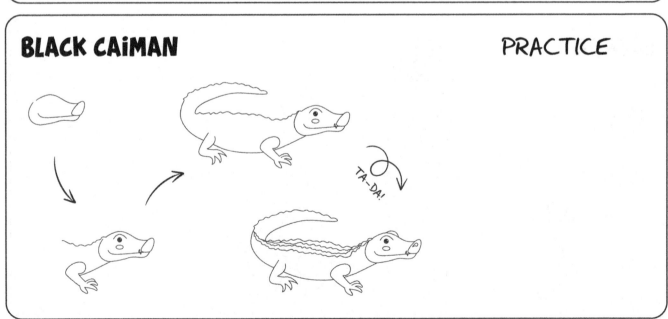

TA-DA!

# TAPIR

# CAPUCHIN MONKEY

# OKAPI

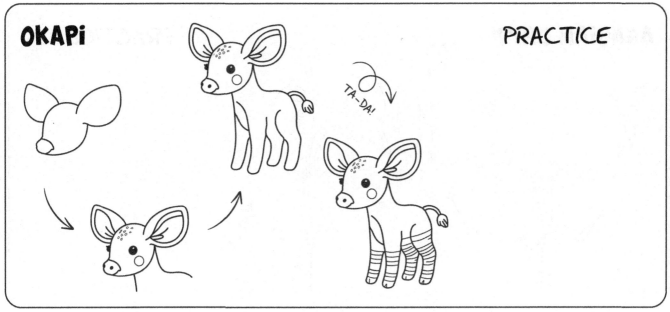

## KOOKABURRA

## AUSTRALIAN TAIPAN

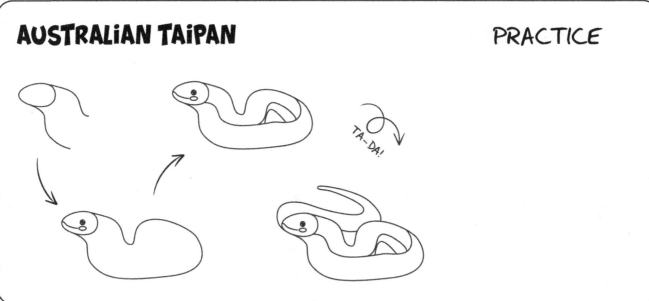

## ARABIAN ORYX

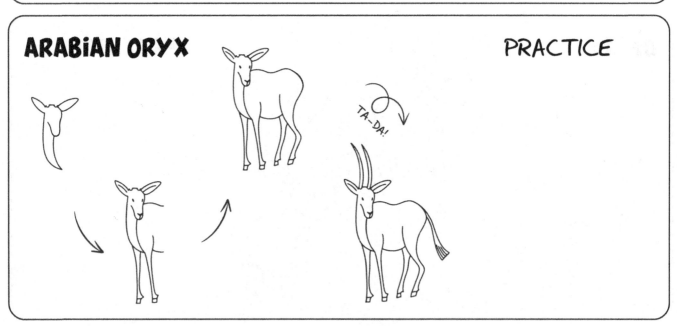

## LEOPARD GECKO

## FENNEC FOX

## PORCUPINE

## CLOUDED LEOPARD

## PROBOSCIS MONKEY

## GHARIAL

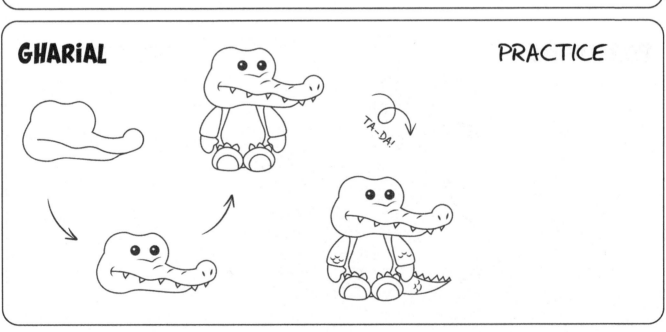

## BACTRIAN CAMEL

TA-DA!

## MONITOR LIZARD

TA-DA!

## GNU GOAT

TA-DA!

# HONEY BADGER

TA-DA!

# AFRICAN PENGIUN

TA-DA!

# AFRICAN BUFFALO

TA-DA!

# WARTHOG

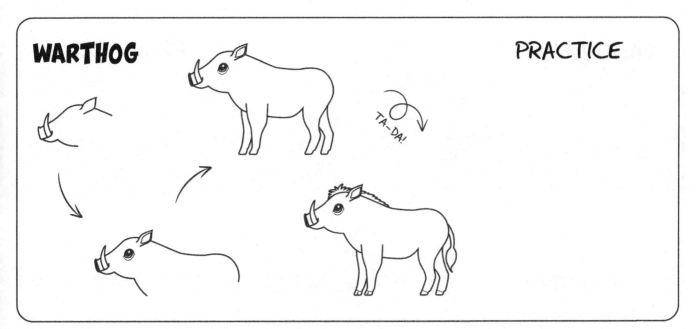

# ANTEATER

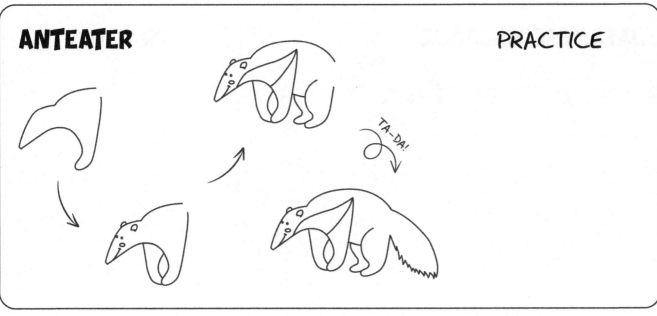

# AFRICAN WILD DOG

## PANGOLIN

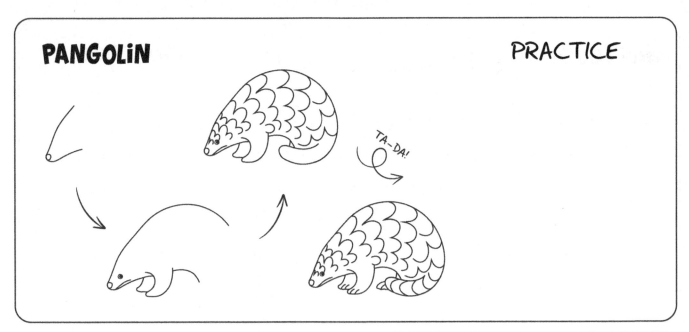

## JAPANESE MACAQUE

## THORNY DEVIL

# CHINCHILLA

# BABOON

# AADVARK

## CAPYBARA

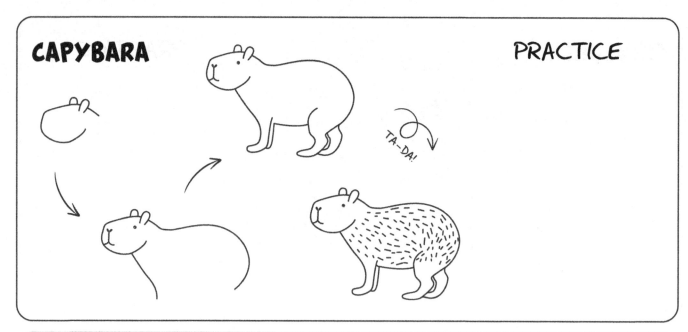

TA-DA!

## GAZELLE

TA-DA!

## EGYPTIAN COBRA

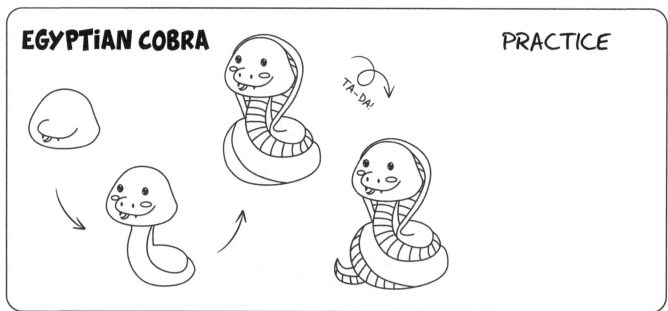

TA-DA!

# JACKAL

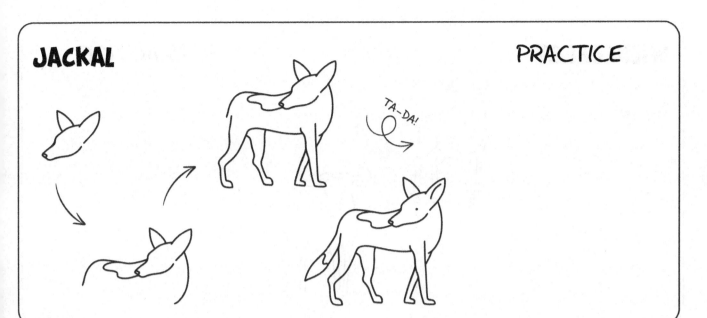

# TOPI

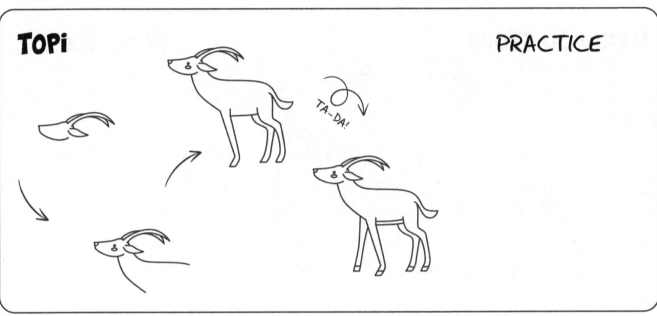

# MANDRiLL

## WILDEBEEST

## MARABOU STORK

## RED PANDA

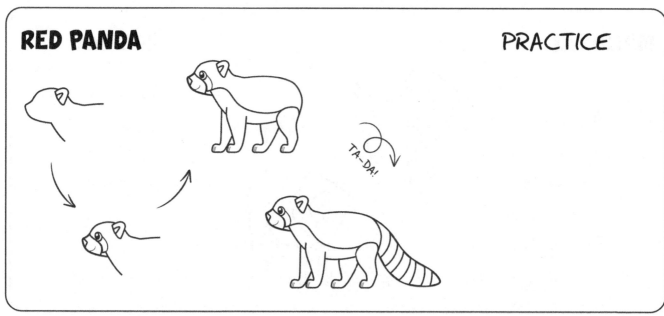

# BiRDS, FLiES AND iNSECTS

## PENGUIN

PRACTICE

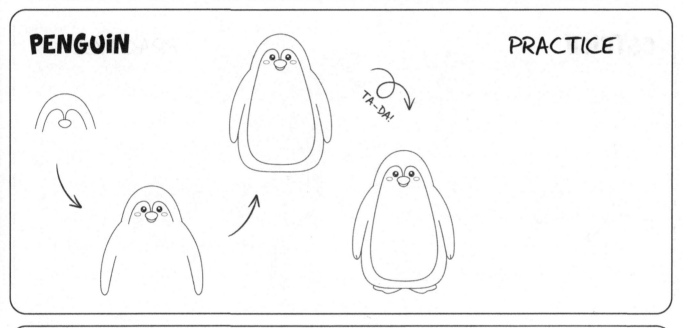

TA-DA!

## OWL

PRACTICE

TA-DA!

## EAGLE

## OSTRICH

## TOUCAN

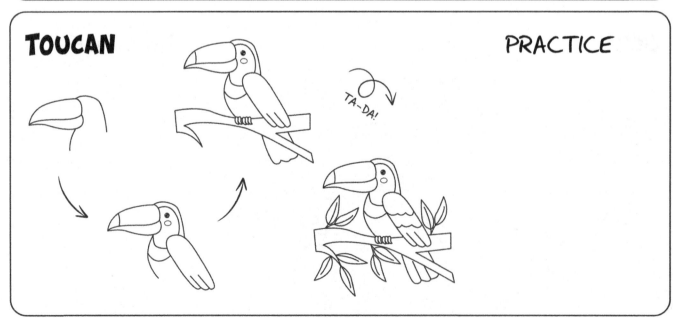

## FLAMINGO

## SWAN

## RAVEN

## STORK

## HAWK

## VULTURE

## PELICAN

## COCKATOO

## EMU

## PEACOCK

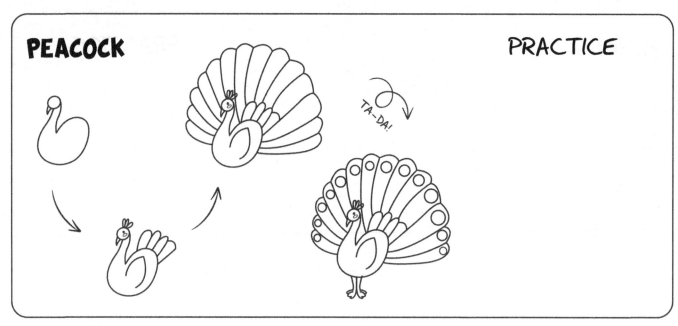

## PiGEON

## KiWi

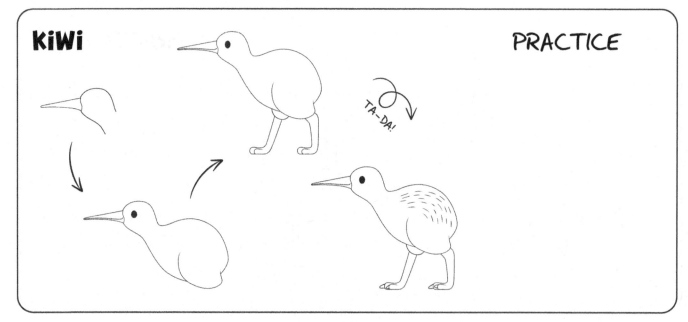

## SEAGULL

## WOODPECKER

## STARLING

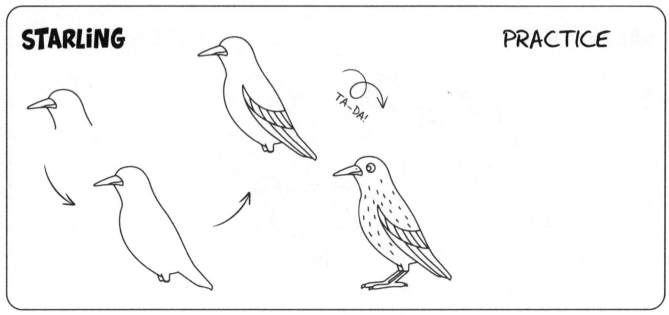

## HERON

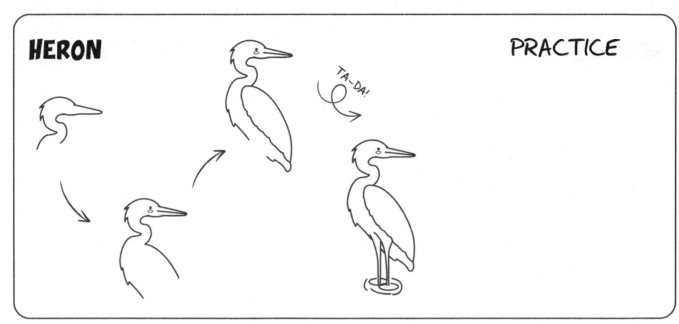

TA-DA!

## ALBATROSS

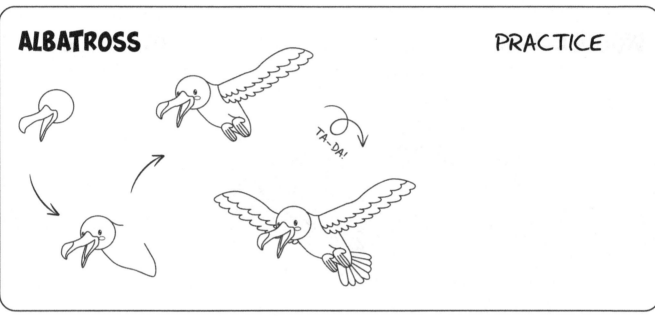

TA-DA!

## SACRED iBiS

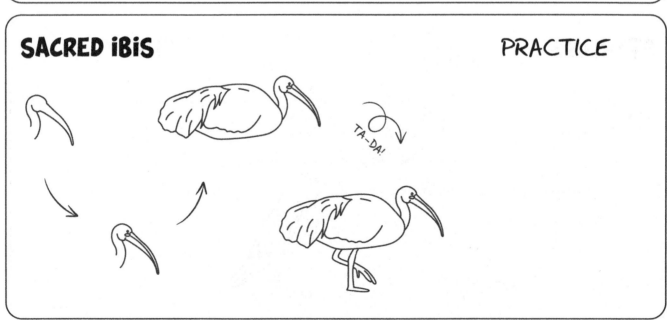

TA-DA!

# HARPY EAGLE

# HUMMINGBIRD

# CORMORANT

## CROW

TA-DA!

## PUFFIN

TA-DA!

## CRANE

TA-DA!

# SPARROW

# BUZZARD

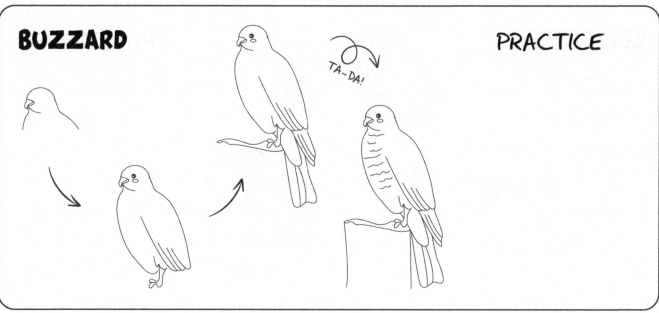

# GUINEAFOWL

## ANDEAN CONDOR

## BEE-EATER

## KiNG PENGiUN

## SECRETARY BIRD

## MAGPIE

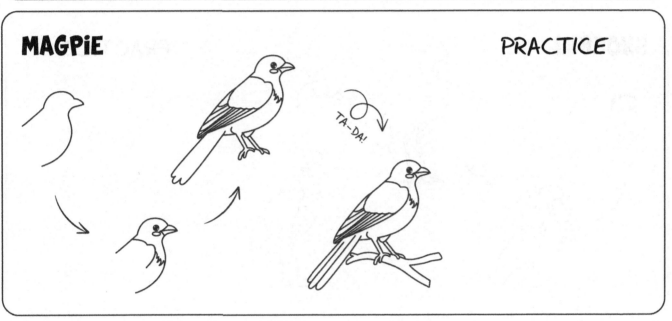

## HORNBILL

# EGRET

# SHOEBILL

# NIGHTINGALE

## BARN SWALLOW

## RED HOOPOE

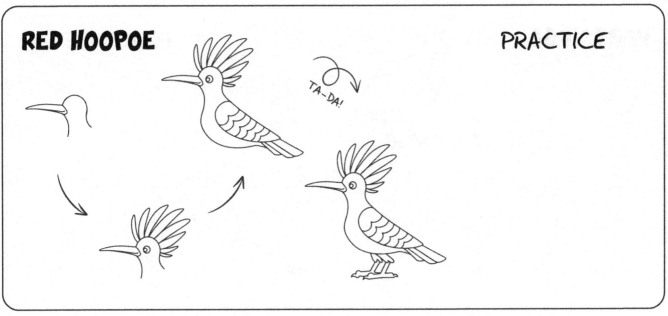

## COMMON KINGFISHER

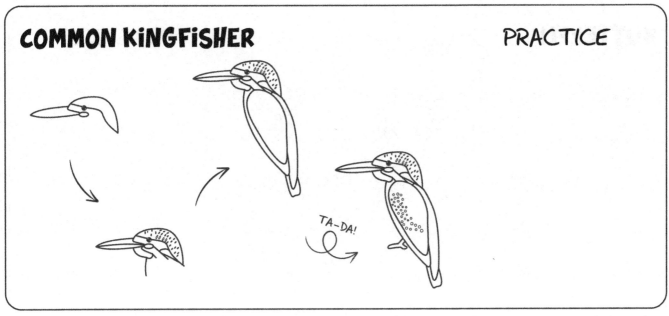

## EURASIAN JAY

## PARTRIDGE

## BUTTERFLY

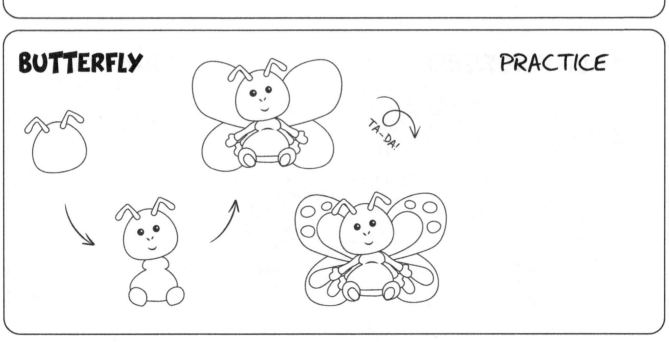

# MOSQUITO

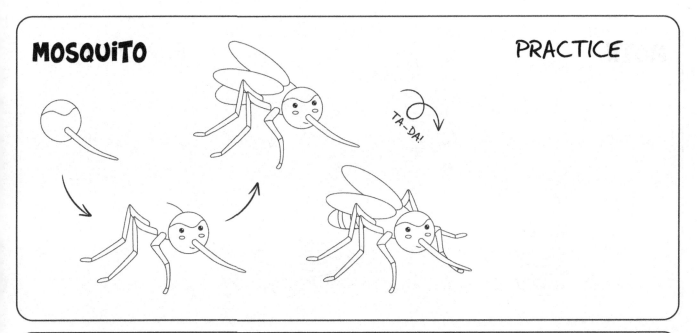

# WASP

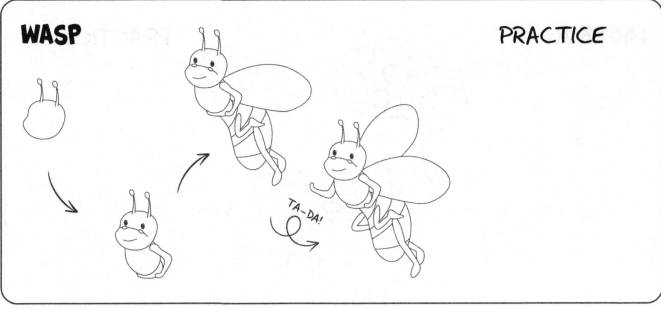

# DRAGONFLY

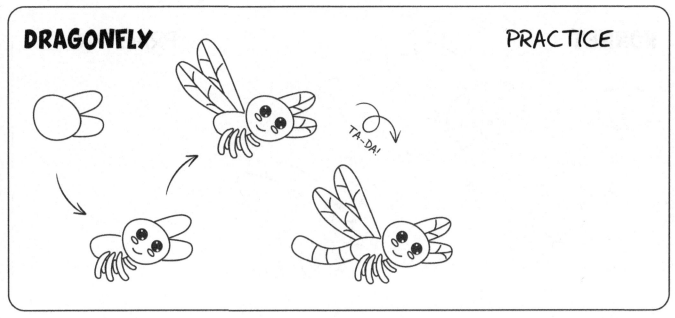

## MOTH

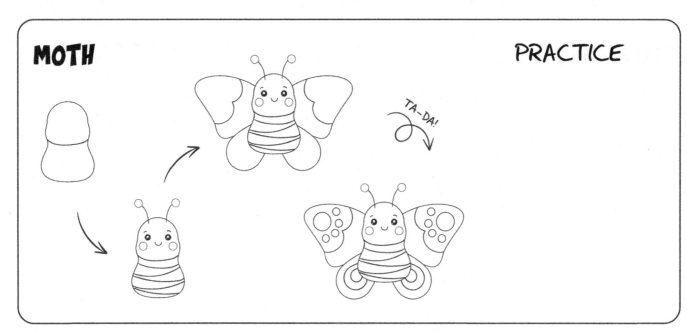

TA-DA!

## LADYBUG

TA-DA!

## HORNET

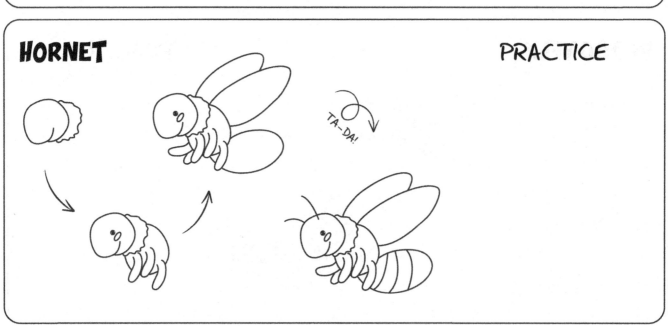

TA-DA!

**FIREFLY**

**MANTIS**

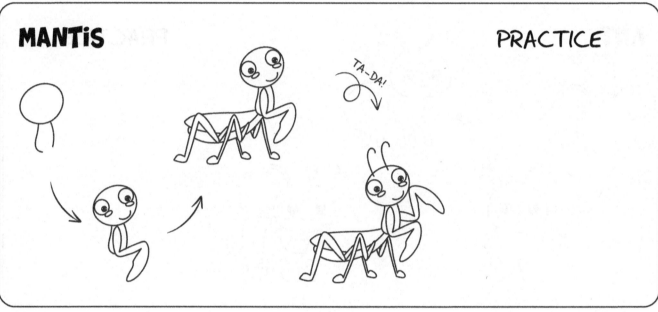

**BAT**

## GRASSHOPPER

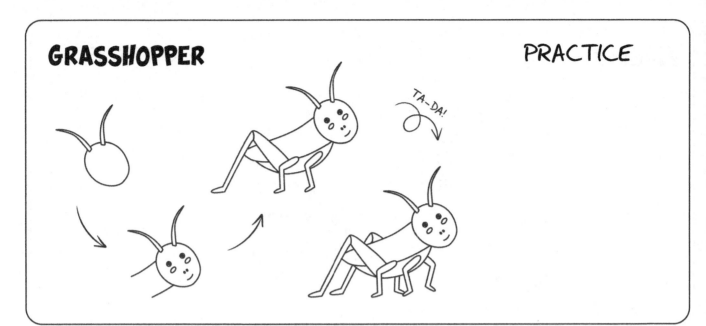

## ANT

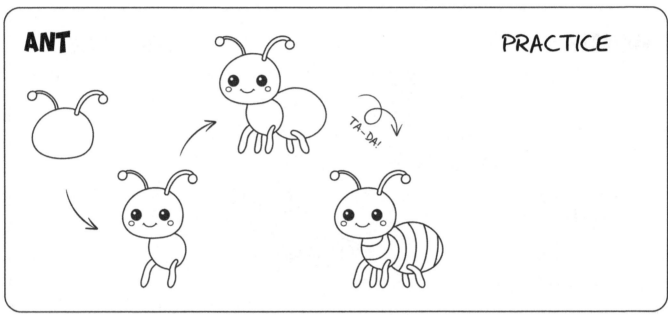

## BEETLE

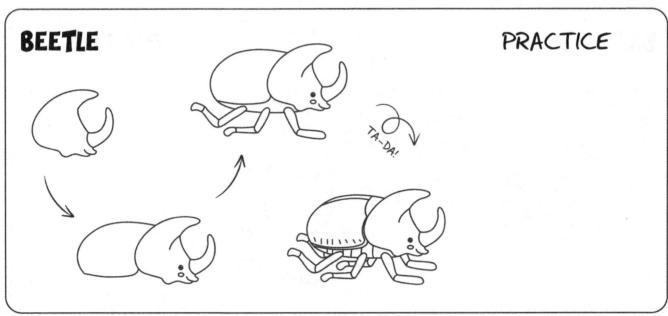

# CRICKET

# TARANTULA

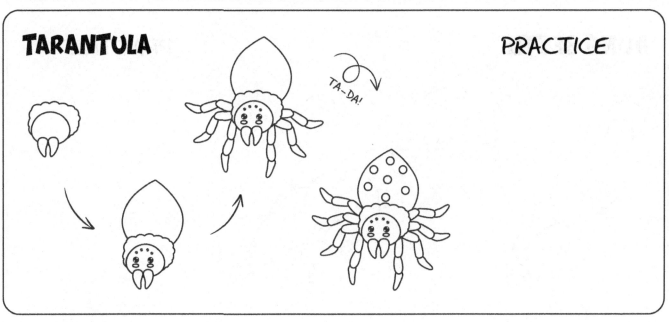

# CATERPILLAR

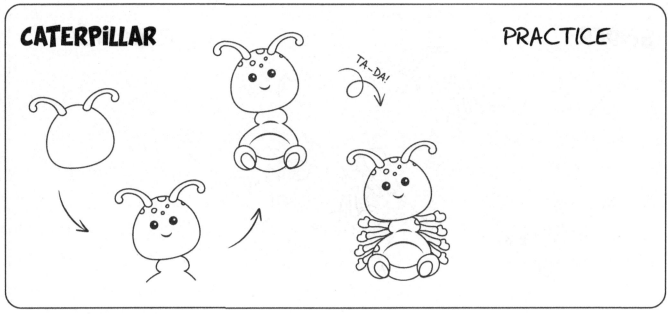

## COCKROACH

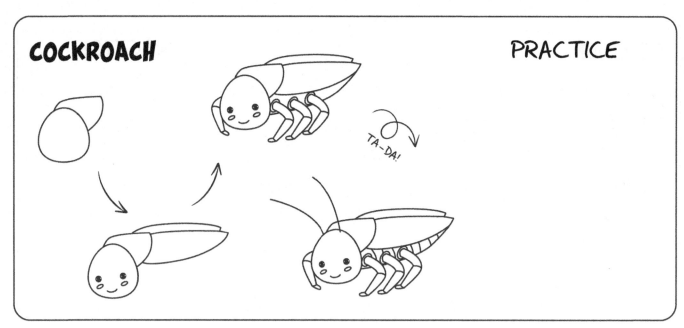

TA-DA!

## DUNG BETTLE

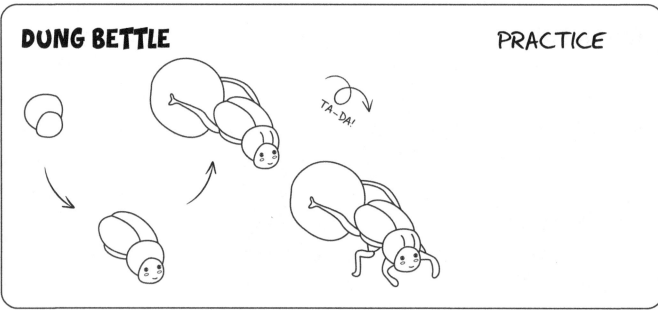

TA-DA!

## SPIDER

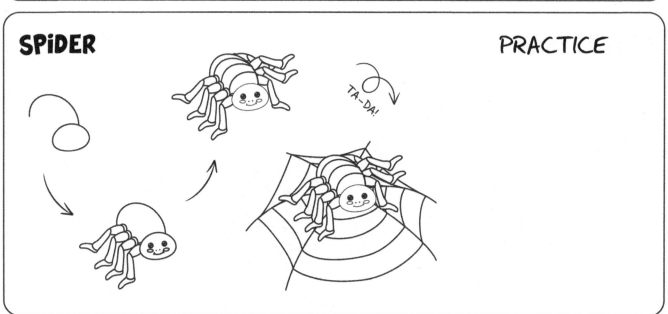

TA-DA!

# MYTHICAL AND FANTASY CREATURES

## UNICORN PRACTICE

TA-DA!

## MERMAID PRACTICE

TA-DA!

## YETI

## PHOENIX

## FAIRY

## PIXIE

## LOCH NESS MONSTER

## PEGASUS

# THUNDERBIRD

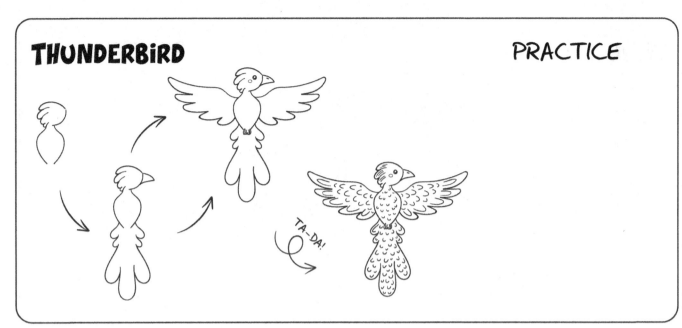

# CENTAUR

# WEREWOLF

# CERBERUS

# DRAGON

# GRiFFiN

## HYDRA

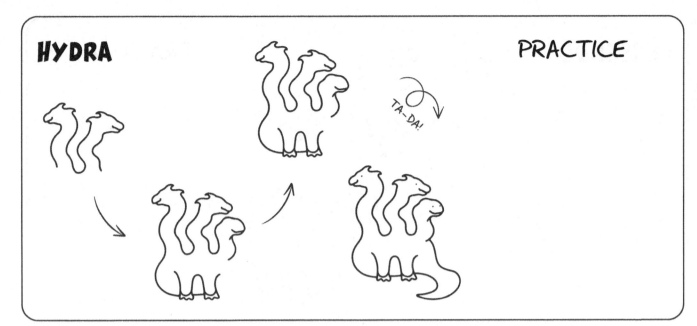

## CHUPACABRA

## KELPIE

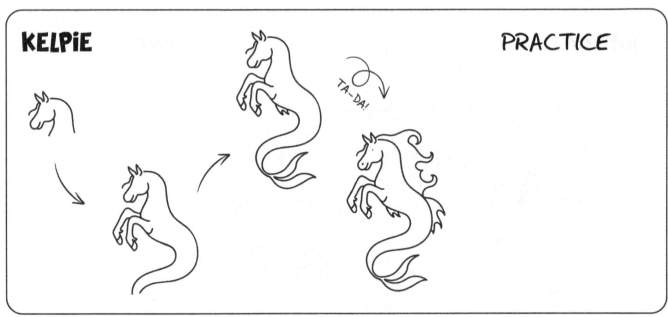

Made in United States
Orlando, FL
11 December 2024

55425193R00063